WHIZZ...

TO

PROMOTION

JOHN MEPHAM

Copyright @ 2013 John Mepham
All rights reserved

Copyright © 2003 John Mebane
All rights reserved

ABOUT THE AUTHOR

When purchasing a book you want to know that the author truly knows the subject being presented to you as an expert's opinion. Therefore, I give a short review of my business career. Please allow me to a little brag!

I started as an office boy with a firm of estate agents in Brighton and soon became a junior negotiator. To increase my knowledge of the business I changed firms and became involved in land acquisition and property development. I sold a site to a firm of developers who were obviously happy with my services. They were building in Luton and Bedford and their estate agents were seeking a manager for their Luton office. They recommended me and I moved my family to Bedfordshire.

A public quoted company that I had known in Brighton became my best client in Bedfordshire. After some ten years they offered me the post of Managing Director of their company. Always willing to grab an opportunity I accepted and my family moved back to Brighton. I remained their Managing Director for just over twenty-two years.

I have no doubt that my extensive business experience gives me the expertise to put **WHIZZ...TO PROMOTION** before you.

THE PROLOGUE

Having purchased this book it can be assumed that you are either thinking about the future and seeking a job or in a job and seeking a step up the career ladder - you are seeking promotion. In either event you have taken the first step and have started to make things happen. You are not prepared to idle your time away day dreaming. It is evident this book was written with ambitious persons like you in mind.

As you read this book you will soon realize that it's aim is to look at objectives which, taken together, will give you a sound background knowledge of what should or should not be done to achieve success/promotion. Each of the twenty objectives draws attention to a specific topic that will help you climb the ladder of success.

I refer to each headed section as an OBJECTIVE. As an example, when referring to section one (You must be in the right job - one that you really care about) it will be referred to as OBJECTIVE ONE.

A book can contain the best advice by a leading expert but unless the reader puts that advice into action it will remain just written words. No more; no less. This old English proverb illustrates that truism. **SOLOMAN MADE A BOOK OF PROVERBS, BUT A BOOK OF PROVERBS NEVER MADE A SOLOMAN.** The moral is well-made. A mere list of words does not help anyone. Be that as it may, we do know that if carefully read, carefully considered and, when appropriate, used in everyday life a true wise list can be very helpful. The list must be used to be beneficial. This is further made plain by my personal motto - **NOTHING HAPPENS UNLESS YOU MAKE IT.** That belief comes out strongly in these pages.

When you think about promotion it is generally considered that another person will move you up the ladder. It follows that humans, not circumstances or things, promote you – but there is a proviso. It is this - you are only promoted if you deserve it. Another person is only likely to use that power if he considers that you desire it and are capable of doing that higher grade job. You see, it all depends on you and only if you really want promotion and work hard towards that end will you be rewarded by another person putting his trust in you. Again - **NOTHING HAPPENS UNLESS YOU MAKE IT.**

The advice and guidance given in these pages can just as well be used with successful results by a sole trader in a profession, business or trade. He has no one to promote him and must promote himself by improving and, possibly, expanding his firm so as to increase his income and standard of living. That shows that every working person seeks promotion one way or another.

A short summary - read carefully these twenty OBJECTIVES and go further than that. Take the ones that personally help you and get your thoughts and actions moving in the right direction. In the final analysis it is only ACTION that will bring you all the success for which you crave.

Before you read these OBJECTIVES there is one cardinal lesson/warning that takes clear precedence over all twenty of them. If this lesson/warning is broken it will, without any doubt, ruin all the benefits that the OBJECTIVES will bring. It is this - you must at all times be honest; for honesty is the backbone of all those who are truly successful and proud of their achievements. Look up the words "honest" and "honesty" in the dictionary. The definitions are illuminating and include truthfulness, decency, good faith, genuineness, sincerity and so on. Remember as you read these OBJECTIVES that you must at all times be honest for, as has been said for generations, honesty is the best policy.

OBJECTIVE ONE – YOU MUST BE IN THE RIGHT JOB – ONE YOU REALLY CARE ABOUT

Most of us consider that money is the be all and end all of life. Few of us stop to think how to achieve the state where money is readily available and you don't have to worry about tomorrow's needs. Those two sentences show the wide gap between action and dreaming. The gap is caused by money being put before all else and it clouds the vision. It is not clearly considered how that happy state can be accomplished. It is assumed - hoped - that the good times will soon arrive without any effort. How wrong can you be?...unless you receive a large inheritance or gamble and win the jackpot. Don't wait for that event to arrive. It's a fair bet that it won't and, in any event, it's beyond your control.

You may be depressed by the last paragraph. Here is the sure cure for that state. To have a chance of gaining success/promotion and a better standard of living you must take control of your life. There is no doubt that work must be the first essential and success will follow if, and only if, you work efficiently and apply your mind one hundred-per-cent to the job. There is no comfortable halfway house. Golf must be taken off the work curriculum. To act and work in the right manner will bring promotion and more promotion... until you get the top job or, and this is an honourable decision, you consider that your existing job suits all your needs or that the next move up is beyond your capabilities – see OBJECTIVE TWO.

Now, you will have to make the acid test. How will you know that the job is not for you? You will soon realize that you are bored; uninterested in the job; have no interest whatsoever in what is happening in the firm generally; dread going into work at nine o'clock every morning and longing to leave at five-thirty or sooner; craving for the weekend and hating Mondays and so it goes on, altogether a miserable life. You will soon take the hint that you ought to be looking for a different job.

What will being in the wrong job do for you? From the above three paragraphs it is clear that being in the wrong job you will lack drive, energy and the desire to seek promotion. All that worry and annoyance of being a square peg in a round hole will destroy any initiative that you possessed. You cannot and will not do your best if the job is not for you. It is like swimming against a tsunami. You just won't get anywhere. You will be washed away.

More to the point, what will be the reaction of your boss? He will soon become aware that you are not enjoying your job and only working to earn a wage to keep body and soul together. You will be banished from his promotion list. The wrong job, the wrong vibes are soon detected by your boss and by colleagues working with you.

The advice of this OBJECTIVE is dramatic but it must be faced. If you are in the wrong job get out NOW. Waiting is likely to increase your dissatisfaction. Find the right job and your interest and drive will revive and promotion will once again be on the agenda.

A caution: You may be in the wrong job with the right firm. If so, before giving notice discuss your dilemma with the boss. Don't act in haste and throw the baby out with the bath water.

OBJECTIVE TWO – YOU MUST KNOW AND APPRECIATE YOUR WEAKNESSES AND LIMITATIONS

Should a person who hates heights become a window cleaner? Should a person who hates mathematics become an accountant? Of course not, as such persons should realise their weaknesses and not attempt a calling that is very likely to be a failure. Likewise, you should know your weaknesses and limitations and steer clear of any job that entails work that, because of a weakness, is not suitable for you. It ought not to be necessary to include that advice in these pages. Sadly, that is not so. Many persons take a job that is not suitable for them and struggle on a day-to-day basis. They are not strong enough in character to admit to themselves or to others that they have bitten off more than they can chew. The result is obvious – a miserable life with little or no hope of any success or promotion. That is a grim warning. The advice is repeated and ties in with the advice given in OBJECTIVE ONE – find a suitable job; use your natural abilities and work hard. Believe in yourself.

One of my favourite authors wrote: **THERE IS NOTHING THAT HELPS A MAN IN CONDUCT THROUGH LIFE THAN A KNOWLEDGE OF HIS OWN CHARACTERISTIC WEAKNESSES (WHICH GUARDED**

AGAINST, BECOME HIS STRENGTH), AS THERE IS NOTHING THAT TENDS TO THE SUCCESS OF A MAN'S TALENTS THAN HIS KNOWING THE LIMITS OF HIS FACULTIES, WHICH ARE THUS CONCENTRATED ON SOME PRACTICABLE OBJECT. ONE MAN CAN DO BUT ONE THING. UNIVERSAL PRETENSIONS END IN NOTHING.** Isn't that a splendid and shrewd quotation? It is a super summing-up of this OBJECTIVE. It is taken from William Hazlett's essay entitled, On the Knowledge of Character. I strongly advise you to read that essay.

If you see a future in your present job with promotion prospects and yet there is a minor weakness that impinges on that goal, it may be possible to eliminate that handicap. As an example, you are an account's assistant, you like the job and can see an excellent future, but, and here is the snag, you are only average at mathematics. You realize that a better grasp of mathematics will better your chance of being promoted. You don't give in. You go to a private tutor for lessons in mathematics – yes, it is a nuisance losing leisure time some evenings and missing golf on a Saturday morning, but you are determined to get ahead in your job. There really is no alternative. Thereafter, as your mathematics improve both your enthusiasm for the job and your chance of promotion gain in strength with your present employer. Better the devil you know...

The lesson of this OBJECTIVE is not difficult to learn. Face up to your weaknesses and limitations and don't let them spoil your advantages. Remember that all humans have advantages and that few use them – you are one of the few.

OBJECTIVE THREE - FROM THIS POINT IN TIME YOU MUST HAVE AN ARDENT AND URGENT DESIRE TO SUCCEED

From this point in time you must change your outlook; that is a (polite) command. Your only working aim is to work towards and to look forward to promotion. There is a Chinese expression that is worth keeping in mind – **CLOSE THE PAST; OPEN THE FUTURE.** Isn't that an admirable way of expressing this OBJECTIVE? That's only six words that convey so much. Of course, you will recall both the good and bad lessons of the past, which is part of your learning curve. It is your experience. You must forget all the doubts, worries and misgivings of past times. It's a tough exercise and it must be accomplished. There is no realistic alternative – only failure. However, there is an important proviso – never forget the LESSONS taught by those mistakes.

This OBJECTIVE is about creating a new way of thinking and working. As a start you know – really know – that success can only be acquired by having the correct thoughts and feelings in your mind. You must condition yourself to that state. Think – of doing more than your best. Think – of achieving success. Think – of getting promotion. Always think in the positive. From positive thoughts positive actions will nearly always flow.

A permanent aim to keep in mind – from today you must have a really strong urge to succeed. Not some vague wishy-washy hope that something beneficial will (suddenly) come along. It won't.

You will have noticed that I am passionate about quotes. They have a habit of remaining in one's memory and are a useful way of recalling actions that must or must not be done. Here is a super quote by President Abraham Lincoln: **YOUR RESOLUTION TO SUCCEED IS MORE IMPORTANT THAN ANY OTHER THING.** Note and keep in mind those three words...<u>resolution to succeed</u>. That is both a quotation and a lesson that must never be forgotten.

Sometimes even the toughest "resolution to succeed" is weakened a little by events. No one can escape the slings and arrows of outrageous fortune. Even in the best summer a violent storm interrupts the ideal weather. Likewise, when all seems to be going well with your working life doubts may come along. When this happens your resolve will be tested. You will look into the future with trepidation. You see yourself with an average job which produces an average wage and little chance of promotion. All the menial tasks are given to you. Most of your friends have enjoyed excellent promotions. You stop work for a moment and think about what might have been. You sigh, "If only..." Silly you, it is too late to alter the past. Your thoughts reluctantly return to the present. You hate being in a situation where you look back in both anger and disappointment.

The only remedy is in your own hands and it is this – brush away all those dismal doubts and get back on the road to success and promotion. You immediately make a firm resolution – I never again want to be in a position where I miserably sigh, "If only..." So, I will from this point in time do more than my best at my job and make absolutely sure that I earn promotion as soon as it is available. That is the positive way to push yourself forward.

It is imperative that you ALWAYS retain that desire to succeed. You have now taken the first vital step. You know what you must do or not do. The first do is that you must persist for, if you fail at that, all is lost. It is said that very little takes place without persistence. Look at all those persons that you know who have been promoted and are well on the way to real success. They all possessed one personal quality – persistence (determination, doggedness, pluck, stubbornness). They did not give up when times got tough, there was no slacking, not (too) much golf...They exercised steady persistence whatever was thrown at them. Don`t envy them, copy them.

OBJECTIVE FOUR – KNOW AND CULTIVATE THOSE WHO HAVE THE POWER TO PROMOTE YOU

Which of these two employees is most likely to get promoted? PERSON A – who is hard working and extremely efficient? He gives his all to his job. He is somewhat shy and keeps very much to himself and only speaks to the boss when needs be. PERSON B – is nearly as good at his job as person A. He is not shy and quietly and calmly displays his abilities to the boss. He makes sure that every good move is known to the boss. Which person is most likely to be promoted?

To know the (possible) answer to that question you must realize that it is a person who makes promotion decisions. Now, that brings a dilemma and may well seem to contradict views already given. Let's get it clear. You must do all that is necessary to get promoted and make absolutely sure that the boss realizes that you are promotion material. If you don't the chance of promotion is less likely and you are wasting your time. The boss's decision will go to a person who has made himself and his usefulness to the business well-known to him. That successful person was cunning and was able to impress the boss by constantly pushing himself and his usefulness to the business.

By the reasoning contained in the last paragraph person B, who quietly cultivated the boss, is likely to be the winner. That shows that in the final analysis it is a person that makes the responsible decision. You see, you may do all that is necessary to warrant promotion but it was your boss who will make the final decision. That is a lesson to learn otherwise you will be frustrated not promoted.

In a nutshell the real lesson to learn is this – if your boss doesn't know of your good work and good qualities he will not have you in the forefront for promotion. Why should he? He is making a vital decision and a wrong one may have dire consequences on his own position. So, make as sure as you can that he gets to know of both you and your plus points. Don't be too obvious. Act naturally and let your actions rather than boastful words speak for you.

You can go further by helping your boss and gaining some useful plus points. Firstly, do not waste his time. He is busier than you. When you speak to him keep it short and let him know precisely what you are saying. Never waffle. Be seen as someone who appreciates that time is a valuable commodity – that is a first-rate plus in a busy workplace. Secondly, protect him and don't let others waste his time. Don't send them off with a curt "he's busy". Be friendly, be helpful and offer to pass on a message. That helpful stance may get back to him and that will be another plus point.

Don't forget that staff talk. Be helpful and extra polite to his secretary. That may well encourage praise. Every little helps...

A summary – in a quiet and polite manner make sure that the boss – and all your superiors – know that you are a person fit in all ways to be promoted. Don't hid your light under a bushel, no one looks under a bushel and you will be unseen and forgotten.

OBJECTIVE FIVE – YOU MUST HAVE A STRONG GENUINE INTEREST IN OTHER PERSONS

From OBJECTIVE FOUR you now realize that persons promote you. It follows as sure as Monday follows Sunday that you must foster a keen interest in other persons. Also, as essential, you must show that you like people, particularly those who have the power to promote you. Of course, you can't like everybody but in the workplace you act and talk as though you do. You may be the best worker in the world and yet when it comes to job promotion you will fall at the first hurdle if the boss doesn't like you, particularly if he feels that you don't like him. The ideal situation is this – show a genuine interest in all in your workplace, reserving just a little extra regard for those superior to you.

From the last paragraph it will be seen that you must have a real interest in all in the workplace. The reason is this – the boss will see and hear how you treat your colleagues and what he gathers will have an influence on his promotion plans. He will want to promote a person who is considerate to all others – both those in higher and lower rank...particularly the latter. To attract the correct attention do not raise your voice when a difficult problem comes along, help the person in trouble and never show up anyone's shortcomings in an aggressive or quarrelsome way. Do give praise when praise is due.

Beware of mishaps. Treat each one as a normal event and help to smooth it over. To act calmly in such circumstances is a valuable plus. It shows an element of leadership material. To show a problem as a troublesome annoying affair (which, of course, it is) that upsets your temper is a big, big minus.

There is an old Spanish proverb – **DON`T SPIT IN THE WELL AS YOU MAY HAVE TO DRINK FROM IT LATER.** In other words, in the context of this OBJECTIVE, don`t bully or laugh at someone`s misfortune it may cause you problems in the future. The aggrieved person may be in a position to "get his own back" at a later date and upset your promotion plans.

Do not be a gossip. It is a dangerous exercise to try to court favour with someone by running down another person. The person listening is likely to reason that he may be the person being denigrated by you in the future. You haven`t gained a friend, you have probably made the listener very distrustful of you and who will avoid you like the plague. Listen to gossip for you may learn something – that is a different exercise.

A useful reminder – if you are interested in others, in their work, families, hobbies, their problems, et al, they will think well of you.

OBJECTIVE SIX – YOU MUST WORK HARD BUT DO NOT RUIN YOUR HEALTH

This is a problem area as many of us push ourselves beyond our mental and/or physical capacities. In many ways it is more dangerous than being lazy or to slack on the job, although the consequences are different.

The division between working and non-working activities can create problems. Hence, work after hours should be avoided if at all possible. That can create another problem; you may be forced by conditions and/or the boss to work longer than normal working hours. If <u>excessive</u> overtime working occurs tell the boss that you are prepared to work overtime, although you must consider your family and other non-working commitments. If put in a pleasant manner and you offer to work a reasonable amount of overtime, he is likely understand.

Why do you work? The answer is to keep your family in the standard of living that suits you. But, here`s the rub, what standard of living should you adopt? Should your existing income dictate the standard or should a more expensive (luxurious) standard be adopted and somehow or other you will find the money to pay for it? If the latter there could be a constant struggle to make ends meet. You will be forced to work harder and harder, even against your own will. Then, the struggle may start to influence your outlook on work, you will become tired, irritable…and that will start to influence your promotion prospects. So, live within your existing income and only increase expenditure and have a higher standard of living as your income increases. Living in that way will avoid many nasty worries. Concentrate on getting promotion, not on worrying about your debts.

The last paragraph does not imply that you should not seek a higher standard of living. It states that for the benefit of your health it is wise to live within your existing income. Always stride for greater things, don`t financially anticipate them.

How do you know that you are overworking? Signs could be that you are always tired from morning to night; that you are touchy and bad tempered; that the satisfaction has gone out of your work and it has become a drudgery; you hate Mondays and so on. It could be that a remark from another person has caused you to consider your workload/lifestyle. For example, "You look very tired". You may not have realized that you are overworking. That adverse comment may be a blessing in disguise. It is said that if you consider that you are working harder than the average person, you are average. However, a hostile remark, your general health, lack of any free time, complaints from your family…will give you a hint that you are burning the candle at both ends. Take the hint and return to a more realistic workload. Overworking causes many distressing problems that hinder the way to promotion.

Overworking can bring worry and tension; those are two of the most frequent causes of ill health at work. Get rid of all work`s worries by immediately facing them. Don`t linger. Discuss worries with the boss and, where pertinent, with your wife or partner. A shared worry is one well on the way to being eradicated. Others close to you may see more than you and may be able to come up with a solution or, at least, some useful advice.

A tip – with individual jobs work as hard as is necessary to efficiently complete a job. You won't gain any plus points by being super-efficient.

OBJECTIVE SEVEN – PROJECT THE CORRECT IMAGE. YOUR APPEARANCE CAN'T BE FAKED

To project the right image is a demanding challenge. Before considering how to create the right image it is essential to realize that the image projected must suit you and your job. Lucky Luciano wouldn't have got away with projecting the image of a vicar. It would have been absurd, pointless and everyone would have seen through that charade. That example clearly shows why the image must be one that is credible.

The correct image to project is your own personality with emphasis on being friendly, helpful and relaxed. Taking these one by one:

BEING FRIENDLY – this state is so well-known that it requires little comment. Look and act as though you are enjoying the meeting. Smile, but don't be false. Don't boast for that just won't work. To give credit where credit is due will earn you many bonus points.

BEING HELPFUL – don't put silly obstacles in the way of agreement. Don't disagree just for the sake of trying to look tough. Don't try to trick a person into doing something he doesn't want to do. Carefully and honestly explain any complex or difficult problem in a clear and easily understood manner. Always listen – as listening can be very helpful (and profitable) to both parties. In all respects make yourself as accommodating as possible.

BEING RELAXED – if you are tense or fidgety it will look as if you are not sure of yourself. It will be an outward sign that you are a little out of your class. Certainly not a person fit to be promoted. So, calm down and enjoy whatever you are doing. A calm and relaxed person helps to promote the right image.

The model image is one that makes you stand out from the

crowd. Be seen. Be heard. Advertise yourself in a modest way. But, do beware, don't become a conceited loudmouth/bighead. You will soon realize where to draw the line. If you don't, other people will soon tell you verbally or by avoiding you. That is the most detested image and will lose you success, promotion...and friends.

What you say is as much part of your personality/image as your actions and looks. Never swear. Don't be in any way offensive. Don't gossip or belittle others. Down be downcast and pessimistic – be cheerful and optimistic. As written earlier, give credit when credit is due as that will show you as a considerate person.

When the opportunity arises do watch successful people and note their attitudes, actions and verbal response to given circumstances.

A summary on image – get it right and you will be remembered for the right reasons; get it wrong and you will be forgotten and avoided for, to you, the wrong reasons. It is essential to project the right image if you want to be on the promotion list. To look efficient is the way to enhance your chance of promotion.

OBJECTIVE EIGHT – EFFICIENT PERSONAL PLANNING IS ESSENTIAL

The overall result of efficient personal planning is that it saves two precious items. TIME – it waits for no one (OBJECTIVE SIXTEEN). It goes and that's that. No recall. No second chance. ENERGY – use up too much energy and you will slow down, everything will take that much longer to do. A tired person is an inefficient one.

It follows that time must be used productively and time at work not wasted on unproductive and useless tasks. As previously stated never expend more energy that is necessary to satisfactory complete a task. To do so is a double whamming – you waste both time and energy.

The last paragraph states why it is crucial to cultivate efficient personal organization. The result of inefficient personal organization is too distressing to contemplate. Just think – it results in a complete muddle, too much hassle trying to catch up on jobs taking too long to complete, being late for appointments, missing important deadlines, trying to put into being ill-conceived and hastily conceited plans... and so it goes on; all causing time and energy to be wasted and stress to be created. A fine disorganized working life...but with some thought it need not be like that.

To help you with your personal organizations consider these suggestions:

ELIMINATE ALL WASTEFUL ACTIVITIES. This will save both time and energy. For example, don't spend too much time surfing the net, e-mailing friends, talking to your colleagues...keep that type of activity for non-working hours such as lunch time. Use working time to work. There may be unavoidable overlap of working/non-working time but correct personal organization will only permit a few overlaps.

CONCENTRATE. Do not flit from one job to another. Save time and energy by completing the job in hand before moving on. This is not always possible but do try. Then, at the end of the day you will not have a host of half-completed jobs. Make it a rule to always concentrate on what you are doing. Remember - when you do that a job is completed quicker than if done when your mind is flashing from one thing to another.

A PRIORITY LIST. Always have a list of jobs that must be completed without any undue delay. Those are the vital jobs that produce business. I call such a list a priority list. Bring it up-to-date before you go home and you will be ready to "get moving" early the next morning. Like the best laid plans the priority list is often ignored when, for example, a really urgent job comes along. That is ok. You still have the list and, hopefully, no job thereon will be overlooked. That is the intension of the list, to keep important jobs before you.

Remember – if a job is out of sight it may well be missed as other jobs come along. It is a truism that everything is urgent. Therefore, carefully note in the priority list the jobs that will, without doubt, both produce business and help your promotion prospects.

In addition to the above there are many ways of improving your personal working habits. Consider – not relying totally on your memory, avoid time wasting meetings, have a neat easy to follow diary and keep it up-to-date, not rushing jobs to cut corners resulting in a poor finished job...as you read those examples you will think of other ways of improving your working habits. Always be on the lookout for improvements, whether you believe it or not, working habits do not stand still. But persons who stand still get left behind and do not prosper.

You will now realize that efficient personal organization can help you in so many ways. Without a shadow of doubt it will be the major aspect that makes or breaks your promotion chances. It is an element in your struggle for efficiency that can be clearly seen by those that matter – the boss and other superiors. Who can't resist admiring a truly well-organised person and sighing in disgust when confronted with a person in a total muddle?

A reminder of your overall aims – to do your job well and to be noticed by those that matter; then, and only then, will promotion be within your grasp. Never forget that efficient personal organization is a plus point when engaged in a promotion interview.

OBJECTIVE NINE – THE TWO RESOURCES NEEDED FOR SUCCESS ARE TO BE ENTHUSIASTIC AND CONFIDENT

Without those two assets it is virtually impossible to gain any promotion or have any worthwhile success. They are fundamental to a successful career and for that reason deserve a separate OBJECTIVE despite having been mentioned elsewhere.

At the start of this OBJECTIVE get clearly in your mind that if you neglect being enthusiastic and confident you will fail. There is no doubt whatsoever that you won't become the managing director of your employer firm unless you are **confident** that one day your dream will come true and that you are sure **(enthusiastic)** that your direction of the firm will take it to new heights. Forget your aspiration for a few minutes and consider what life would be like without enthusiasm and confidence.

NO ENTHUSIASM – you are aimlessly drifting with no ambition or conviction. No get-up-and-go drive and very little, if any, excitement in your working day. Longing for the end of each working day and dreading the start of tomorrow.

NO CONFIDENCE – scared to act for fear of failure. You are uncertain and dithering with a dread of meeting successful, or even unsuccessful, people. You think that you know that nothing will go right.

From those two short rundowns (an apt word!) you will be convinced that lacking those two assets you need not even think about gaining success/promotion. You have come to the correct conclusion and made a splendid decision and now know that you MUST cultivate being both enthusiastic and confident.

The last three paragraphs give the negatives; now for the positives.

BEING ENTHUSIASTIC is having a strong drive to succeed, being excited that you have a beneficial aim, wanting to achieve a desired goal, doing all that is possible – and more – to get that promotion. Once you are really enthusiastic you will never again want to be a stick-in-the-mud. You will want to grab every opportunity on the road to promotion and, like perpetual motion you will be difficult to stop.

BEING CONFIDENT is having trust in yourself and your aims and knowing that you will able to surmount any difficulty on the way.

Contemplate those positive attitudes. Keep them well in mind and put the negative ones in the bin marked "Not now needed; replaced by experience".

ON BEING ENTHUSIASTIC – Firstly, a quote – **ENTHUSIASTS ARE FIGHTERS. THEY HAVE FORTITUDE. THEY HAVE STAYING QUALITIES. ENTHUSIASM IS AT THE BOTTOM OF ALL PROGRESS. WITH IT THERE IS ACCOMPLISHMENT; WITHOUT IT THERE ARE ONLY ALIBIS.** Now, that quote teaches many aspects of enthusiasm. It is a quote by that great industrialist Henry Ford. Put the sentiments expressed in it in your memory bank and never forget them.

It is essential to show enthusiasm in your job and that is the way to successfully seek promotion. Your boss will warm to someone who is really enthusiastic (and confident). Enjoy your job. Eagerly do even the most menial task to the best of your ability. Arrive at the workplace on time – maybe a little earlier! Don`t be too eager to leave on time. Willingly work (reasonable) spells of overtime as necessary or when asked. In other words prepare yourself for that promotion interview.

ON BEING CONFIDENT – Dismiss all negative thoughts and immediately replace with positive ones. Only by being positive can you remain confident. When a negative thought creeps in your confidence will become a little less sound. So, dismiss that negative intruder immediately. Don`t give it a chance to upset your confidence. Remember – confidence is looking ahead in a hopeful positive manner; looking forward to a future that you KNOW will be a rosy one. You know – really know – that you have the ability needed to successfully do the tasks ahead. Now, that last sentence brings to light a necessary. It is this – you will only have a true unshakeable ability if you REALLY know your job. You can`t kid yourself. In the final analysis you must really know all aspects of your job and confidence will shine through. Then you will be able to say to yourself with utter conviction and confidence – "Promotion here I come."

**ENTHUSIASM + CONFIDENCE
= PROMOTION**

OBJECTIVE TEN – A SUCCESSFUL PERSON IS WELL-INFORMED ON MATTERS RELATING TO HIS WORK AND TO GENERAL EVERYDAY AFFAIRS. HE MUST HAVE A GOOD ALL-ROUND KNOWLEDGE OF WHAT`S GOING ON

Here is a super quote to start this OBJECTIVE. **CHANCE FAVOURS THE PREPARED MIND,** said Louis Pasteur. It puts in a nutshell, in just five words the theme of this OBJECTIVE. In the context of being promoted it means that if you are well-informed, especially about your job and the firm that employs you, you will be high on the list when promotions are considered. That is being a little pessimistic for we know that there is not just a chance of promotion for the well-informed, it is a certainty.

You must learn all that is possible about your employers and your own particular job within the firm. You will in the natural course of events learn much as you work. Additionally, do not be shy of asking the boss or anyone else when you come across a problem that needs an explanation. That will not only help you to gain valuable knowledge and experience, it will vividly show your keenness to progress. It will be a big plus to let your boss know of your intention to learn all about the business. That will help to focus his attention on you.

With certain jobs it is possible to belong to a professional body, a trade association or similar. It is essential to join for that shows a genuine commitment to both your job and your employers. Furthermore, such bodies issue journals, trade paper, et al. These together with general magazines that impinge on your job should be avidly read. They are a splendid source of technical and general information. You can`t read enough about the enterprise in which you work.

A useful reminder - by questioning, reading and studying you will learn much about the industry in which you work and about your own specific job; by doing so you will enhance your chance of being noticed and promoted.

It is essential to know what is happening in the world beyond your job. Events away from the workplace can have a devastating impact on both your employers and on your own job. The impact could be beneficial or detrimental. In either event you should know what is happening for you may have to adjust your actions and outlook to suit changing times. Working conditions, income, spending habits...would all benefit from a boom or suffer in a slump. So, as far as is possible be prepared. However, don`t panic if the news suggests bad times, don`t get over confident on the hope of future boom times. Be realistic and don`t do anything on a rumour. Work on; watch conditions on a day-to-day basis. Remember - the worse rarely happens but that doesn`t mean that you completely ignore possible changes in the future. If it seems that trade will be hard to come by in the future, carefully trim your outgoings (and work harder). If present conditions suggest a possible boom, prepare to work even harder so as to reap any benefits that you can scoop. You see, whatever the conditions prepare to work harder! - See OBJECTIVE - 6.

A comforting thought - **the worse rarely happens**.

It is not difficult or too time-consuming to acquire a general idea of what`s happening in the world around you. A wealth of information can be gained by listening to the news and news programmes on the car radio. National and local newspapers are another useful source. It is not necessary to fully read them, just glance at the headlines and read the news under those that suggest the contents may be useful to know. When you hear or see an item that is of real interest you can research for additional information.

OBJECTIVE 11 - NEVER FORGET THAT GOOD MANNERS ARE NOT ONLY FOR USE IN THE GOOD TIMES. GOOD BEHAVIOUR IS CRUCIAL TO HELP YOU CALM DOWN WHEN BAD TIMES COME ALONG.

Good manners have distinct benefits. Firstly, the right image is created and you are shown in a pleasing light (OBJECTIVE - 7). In itself that is excellent. You are displaying promotion assets. Secondly, good manners create a calming influence on those that you meet - the more aggressive ones are generally inclined to be cowards and sense that behind calm demure is a determined person. So, hating to face a determined person they tend to calm down. Very few persons want to appear bad-mannered and/or unreasonable when faced by a well-mannered and reasonable person. So, your calm manner will help to spike someone's aggressive stance and that must be a plus point.

Good manners are all part of creating the right image, but it goes further than that. A decent image can be lost in a flash if you are rude or offhand. This is especially dangerous if the recipient is the boss. An act of bad-manners can, and generally does, happen in a flash and, bang, the damage is done. No recall. By apologising you may think (a pious hope) that you have been forgiven. As a rule it is not that easy. Nevertheless, you must say "sorry" and, even after a display of regret, the stigma may remain. Think - who will I upset if I'm rude, offhand or use bad language? Answer - almost certainly another person who is more than likely to pay you back sooner or later. You have made yourself a marked man. Aggrieved persons, like elephants, never forget.

There are so many ways of being bad-mannered. Even some quite small and insignificant actions or a few words may be taken as an offence. As an example, not answering his "good morning", letting the door swing back into his face, interrupting when he is talking to someone else...little things, but annoying and show that you are not thinking of other persons. Such an act will linger in the other person's mind and you will be labelled as a bad-mannered and ill-considerate person. Don't forget that all these little faults build up in the aggrieved person's mind.

Saying a genuine "sorry" immediately after the offence may help to lessen the damage done. It is an admission that you acted wrongly. It implies that you are not bad-mannered for you are apologising for a slip of the tongue or whatever. It was a one-off occasion and you are really sorry. You must hope that it wipes away your misdeed. You can never be sure. Also, it shows that you don't want to upset any person. It is a sign that you want to get back onto good terms with him – "let's forget my mistake". Ok, that might help now, but will, as discussed earlier, your misdeed really be forgotten? Better to control yourself, have no need to apologise and, hence, have no possible blot on the future.

A useful tip - When you are bad-mannered and lose your temper who really suffers? You fume and that harms your blood pressure and, if repeated on many occasions, could damage your heart. That little piece of information will, it is hoped, help you to remain good tempered. Keep thinking - being ill tempered will harm ME and others will turn against me. That is another double whamming.

Here is a simple way to avoid being bad-mannered - practise being good mannered. That's easier said than done! When you sense that another person's actions or words may lead you to an ill-conceived outburst don't become involved. Walk away or stop and reply in a pleasant low-key manner. You can still be firm and contradict his assertions in a calm and polite way. I often say, "You don't really mean that, do you? Shall we forget it and start again?" Firmly show that you are not going to engage in a row or slanging match. That nearly always brings an unpleasant situation under control.

Here is a piece of information that reinforces the import of this OBJECTIVE. More employees lose their jobs by personality conflict than by being inferior at their work. That confirms that you must be both calm and good mannered/tempered in an endeavour to remain friendly and businesslike with all in your workplace from the boss downwards. Don't let a poor personal disposition ruin your promotion prospects.

GOOD MANNERS HELP YOUR PROMOTION PROSPECTS

OBJECTIVE 12 - NEVER WASTE ENERGY - WASTED ENERGY MEANS LESS STAMINA FOR ESSENTIAL WORK

How often as your work ends have you wished that you had just a little more energy to complete an important job? You were weary and cast the job aside for completion tomorrow. I bet the answer to that (dreaded) question is "very often". If you had looked back over that specific day you would possibly have found a way of saving some energy. However, as the day progressed you did not realise that energy was "leaking away". Your tired body and tired mind took orders from a tired brain and you drifted pointlessly on. You didn't realise that you were your own worst enemy.

Unless you carefully conserve energy it will slowly and surely leak away. Think of a leaking water pipe, unless repaired it will leak until the water supply is turned off. To conserve energy is a difficult task, yet it must be accomplished. Carefully consider the following advice and, when practicable, use it in your working day to slow down the leakage of energy. A leaking water pipe relies on humans to solve its problem, you are lucky for you have the remedies to solve loss of energy in your own hands.

1 - The saving of energy will be made by efficient personal organisation. Therefore, read again OBJECTIVE - 8. Do more than re-read it, put the ideas into action. It can't be reiterated too often that efficient personal organisation is the surest way to save energy.

2 - There is no doubt that energy is lost by worry (OBJECTIVE-19). Don't look back and worry about yesterday. No amount of worrying will alter the past. If you did your best - as you are now doing - there is little to worry about. Worry is a form of fear. You worry - about the meeting that you have to attend in an hour's time, about putting last month's sales figures to your Sales Director tomorrow, about the meeting with your largest customer next Friday... and so it goes on, you worry about everything. You fear this,

that and the other. Rid yourself of worry and of fear by concentrating on what you are doing today. That is the surest way to lessen worry for, by doing so, you will not have the time to do other than what you are doing today. Crowd it out of your timetable. That advice is easy to write - but do try it and you will realise that it is a sure remedy.

Of course, work is not the only way to beat worry and fear. Consider a particular worry or fear, analyse it, take whatever action is necessary to rid yourself of it, forget it and push on. You see, action must be taken. Don't let the problem fester in your mind. That will cause all sorts of trouble, not least loss of energy, drive, et al. Get it out in the open. Be ruthless and destroy it before it destroys you. This is not easy to do so get help from the boss, the wife/partner and any other person who is in a position to help and whom you can trust.

We all worry about the future. Well, a certain degree of worry is permissible - only a little. You are looking after the future today by doing your best to obtain promotion and that is the way to secure satisfactory and happy days to come. Your aim is for better times and that should not cause worry or fear. The answer is to feel confident because you KNOW - really know and not a false assumption - that you have positively and thoroughly mastered your job, carefully planned the way ahead and are reading this book. You are steadily moving towards promotion.

3 - Never put more energy into any action that is necessary. As an example, don't run as those few seconds saved is energy lost (wasted), don't stand when you can sit, never shout or get het up for that's energy lost through the mouth, don't daydream for that will take your mind off the job and it will take longer to complete...

4 - If you make a mistake you will worry and that, as you now know, burns up energy. To cut that energy losses to a minimum immediately admit your error and, if possible,

put it right. No ifs, no buts, admit it without any petty or silly qualifications. If it involves others admit your problem to them and ask for their help to remedy it. Never try to pass the blame to another person but if another person is genuinely involved discuss on the basis "...sorry, but WE have a problem, let's look at this together...". You can't permanently hide an error or mistake, the longer you try to do so the bigger and more damaging the result will be. To summarise - get the problem into the open, get it out of your mind, (if possible) remedy it and move swiftly on.

5 - When times are difficult you will use extra energy as a car uses more petrol when climbing a steep hill. The car can't slow down and save petrol, it must chug on or stop. You have a remedy. Get yourself accustomed to more difficult conditions and plan your work accordingly.

6 - Relax. That is not easy when a difficult, complicated or unusual task or circumstances hit you. Step back from the task and take a few minutes off. Go for a gentle stroll, think of a peaceful countryside or seaside scene which is known and adored by you, talk the problem over with a friend...get back to a relaxed state and tackle the dilemma. By doing this you have removed yourself from the scene of the difficulty, refreshed yourself and returned in a different and more relaxed state of mind.

7 - After work do something entirely different to the day job. That will get your thoughts away from the trials and worries of work and will help to recharge the batteries. It will help if your hobby is physical like playing golf, attending to the garden, jogging, walking...those and similar activities will get you into another world. Of course, those and similar activities use up energy, but it is a different energy to that used in the day job. Have you noticed that that when you arrive on the first tee at six o'clock in the evening all the tiredness and jangled nerves of the working day melt away? It's a different world, a new challenge and pleasant scenery.

The cure for loss of energy is so easy to prescribe, yet it is so difficult to eradicate. You will soon get to know your own energy limits. You will know when to slow down, when to have a short break or when to walk away and take a longer break. Don't be shy of using these palliates for the energy being lost is yours. Get this control of energy right and you will find that you are retaining more energy than in the past.

OBJECTIVE 13 - WITHOUT ACTION NOTHING HAPPENS, FOR ONLY "DOERS" ARE ACHIEVERS

For many years my personal motto has been **NOTHING HAPPENS UNLESS YOU MAKE IT** and that is true in all walks of life. It is more accurate to say that nothing good happens unless you make it. Really bad events come along whether you like it or not. However, such qualifications added to a motto make it unwieldy and not so easy to recall. A few crisp words are the ideal motto. My motto has a place in your life. You - and only you - will make (good) things happen. No one else will help you for they are all fighting their own battles. The first lesson of this OBJECTIVE is do nothing or very little to get promotion and you will look back and sigh, "If only...". Those two dreaded words which, in that context, should never be allowed to pass your lips.

Think of all the real achievers that you know. Don't you see one common factor? They are all hardworking persons whom, from the start of their careers, knew - really knew - that they had to help themselves. Like a writer who starts with a plot or a few ideas and a blank sheet of paper and little else, the achiever-to-be starts with a few ideas (perhaps only one) and the will to put it into action. The thought with the greatest influence on any career is **THAT NOTHING UNLESS YOU MAKE IT** That must be the kingpin of your own thinking. Never for one moment forget that that you are out there on your own. This applies whether you are an employee or self-employed.

Never forget that whether you have hundreds of friends or only one in the final analysis, where work/business/money is concerned it is you versus the rest.

In my early days as a junior office boy/negotiator with a firm of estate agents I noticed that most other negotiators sat waiting for the telephone to ring. To me that seemed like a waste of prime selling time. I used my own system of calling either by telephone or a personal call on six applicants each day. Of course, this was before the computer, internet, et al. took over our jobs. It proved a worthwhile and profitable exercise. I not only increased my property sales, I was able to obtain instructions to sell houses from applicants whom I contacted and had already purchased another house. That was a good two prong success which illustrates that **NOTHING HAPPENS UNLESS YOU MAKE IT.** It was at that stage of my career that I put together that motto. I have used it ever since. Make sure that you have a motto that will help you in your career.

A summary - Constantly recall that achievers are "doers" and that you will only follow in their footsteps if - and only if - YOU make things happen

OBJECTIVE 14 - YOU MUST THINK POSITIVELY, FOR ONLY POSITIVE THINKING IS THE WAY TO THE CORRCT SOLUTION

Positive thinking is putting all negative and unrelated thoughts in the background and concentrating on the subject being considered. It is using a clear brain/mind to seek out the right solutions. It is being precise, emphatic, certain, definite...and admitting to no doubts. That is a tough description of positive thinking but it is necessary, for to achieve it you must be all of those attributes mentioned - and more. It is too easy to say, "don`t be negative". Positive thinking is the ideal state that will help you to gain promotion more than any other action or display. It is absolutely concentrating on the matter in hand - that is, your job; and thinking and talking about it in a constructive (positive) way. Of course, the ideal state rarely exists and you must work very hard to get anywhere near it.

Positive thinking will be needed to solve individual problems and it is positive thinking that helps you to arrive at the correct solution thereto. To half consider a problem with the other half of you thinking about another problem, tomorrow`s golf match or whatever will without any doubt not help you to reach the right answer. Positive thinking is concentrating one-hundred-per-cent on the matter in hand and seeking out all angles that are likely to help you reach the right answer. You will be too busy to be negative.

To arrive at the correct solution you must make-up your mind, you must not let your brain waffle. You must be firm and clear as you cogitate on a problem. Now, that is not as difficult as it may seem, although it does need careful preparation. Consider these suggestions:

1 Write down the problem on paper. List the pros and cons on the known facts; ignore rumours and wild illogical untruths. That exercise will concentrate the mind and help to draw it in the right direction. That is a good start to positive thinking - you have the known facts in black and white. Try to summarise in a single sentence the problem. Again, that will concentrate the mind and help to do away with all the minor and irrelevant worries. You should now have before you the problem shorn of all unnecessary "ifs" and "buts".

2 Look at each suggestion implied by each of the listed pros and cons. Isolate the credible solutions and keep the final selection to the two most likely solutions. If there is a third really likely suggested solution retain it with the other two.

3 Consider in detail the isolated solutions against the problem. Look at each with what I call "the five questions that the final solution has to stand up to". Against each isolated solution ask, as applicable, who, how, what, why and

where? Gradually the final solution will come to light. Do remember that you must have faith in the final solution. Don't adopt a final solution because it looks right if you have any doubts. If you don't have faith in the final answer it is unlikely to work for you.

4 Before using the solution check it once more against the pros and cons that you listed. This is the "belt and braces" final check.

Of course, it will not be feasible to use the above method of selection in all circumstances. However, the general idea outlined will help you to think through solutions. It is a guide which you can adapt to suit your own style of working.

Positive thinking can be helped by using experience from the past. You will find that many situations faced today have, in some way or another, cropped up in the past. Think back and consider the solution that you then used. Even if that is not suitable for today's problem you will be considering other ways of solving problems and new ideas may emerge. All the time that you are thinking positively you will be solving problems, creating new ideas and moving forward. A positive thinking person is invariably ahead of competitors. He is surely moving towards promotion.

OBJECTIVES 15 - NEW IDEAS ARE THE LIFE BLOOD OF BUSINESS. PEOPLE APPRECIATE ONE WHO SEEKS NEW WAYS ON IMPROVING THE EVERYDAY

What is a new idea? It can be defined as an intellectual action which is likely to produce an alternative way of performing an operation or creating a brand new product or service. It is commonly called a "brainwave"; it is an original thought. It is helpful to remember that every advance, every new gadget, every new way of doing things...sprang from a thought (idea) which flashed though the mind of a person just like you. It must not be forgotten that a person activated that thought. Again, we come back to - nothing happens unless you make it. Even something as spirited as a new idea is of no use whatsoever until it is grabbed, considered and kick-started by a person.

It is a common fallacy that there is nothing new under the sun, that everything has already been invented. Think for a moment, years ago - who would have dreamed of computers, the Internet, the mobile `phone, et al? You see, there is a constant stream of new inventions always coming along. Of course, all are not of the same significance as the three just listed. Each of us has an opportunity of creating something new or, perhaps more likely, a better way of doing a task. We can`t all invent a world shattering innovation. We can improve our own way of working by seeking less expensive and/or time-saving ways of doing our everyday tasks. You may hit on an idea that could be used commercially, although this OBJECTIVE relates to ideas that could be used to help both your employer and yourself to prosper. If you don`t keep up-to-date you will very soon fall behind the crowd and all hopes of success will fail. Hence, help yourself by assisting your employer to seek both improved and new methods.

The guide to finding new ideas is this - always look for the unknown factor. Search for an area to exploit. A good example is an area of your work that looks, and possibly is, out-of-date. Consider an area which, for some reason or another, is not as profitable as it should be or is badly run and always throwing up problems. Those last three words illustrate a source for investigation. A procedure which is always breaking down is an area to explore - it is ripe for improvement. Think of an idea to remedy the deficiency. Often the cause is pure inefficiency either caused by an old and weak system or by the persons running the system being badly trained, poorly supervised or just plain lazy. Solve that one and you will be truly marked as promotion material by a grateful boss.

How do you handle a new idea in your workplace?

You are sitting in your workplace and out-of-the-blue you have a brainwave. There is a new (better) way of doing a task that you do several times a day. You should proceed in this manner:

1 Keep testing the idea to make sure that it really does do the job quicker and more efficiently. Will it save money? When reasonably satisfied move to stage two.

2 Is it realistic to think that the existing job could be adapted to the new idea? Don't let your enthusiasm fool you. Do be realistic. Consider the likely savings in cost, although you may not have the experience to come to a decision on this score (see below). If you do believe that it is a practical proposition move to stage three.

3 Now is the time to put the idea to the boss. Give as complete a picture as is possible. Admit that you are not sure of certain elements, particularly costings and you would appreciate his views. Don't be shy of being turned down, even an abortive attempt to introduce a new way of working shows both interest and initiative. That is a big plus and shows promotion qualities. A warning/reminder - don't forget that the idea MUST be carefully considered as suggested in (1) and (2) above. It must only be put to the boss if you really do consider it a workable idea. Don't waste your boss's time. A scatterbrain idea is not promotion material, quite the reverse!

OBJECTIVE 16 - THE GOLDEN RULE - NEVER WASTE WORKING TIME

You will have noticed that this OBJECTIVE says never waste WORKING time. Notice the emphasis. What you do outside working time is entirely up to you and your family. It is a family/relaxing time and whether you play golf, go walking, collect postage stamps, play the trumpet...that's your choice.

An excellent start to this OBJECTIVE is a Himalayan proverb, one that I adore. It is this – **HUMANS SAY THAT TIME PASSES; TIME SAYS THAT HUMANS PASS.** Isn't that so true, no prize for guessing the winner. That proverb will put you in the right mood for the rest of this chapter. Its message is that time quickly passes. Act whilst you are able!

Nowadays we have to recycle nearly everything but, sadly, we can't recycle time. It comes, it's here, it's gone. Or, to put it in a more useful way - it comes, it's here and you must use it wisely, it's gone and you will happily look back on a worthwhile past or you will keep sighing, "If only...", depending on how you used all your yesterdays. You do not notice time passing, it passes so quickly. The future is soon today, today is very soon tomorrow...and so it speeds silently and unnoticed away. How you use time is entirely in your hands. The choice is yours but never forget that there is no second chance.

From the above comments on time you will realise that working time must be conserved and used wisely. It must not be allowed to slip away whilst you rest on your laurels. For, if that is allowed to happen - or, happens by default - you will soon have no laurels to rest on.

To make the most of your working time consider the following recommendations. Some of these have been mentioned in other OBJECTIVES and are listed under this one so that you realise many possible ways of conserving time. There are many other ways of doing so. As you use those listed hereunder you will think of other ways that suit your own modus operandi.

    1 The overall objective is to make sure that you do efficiently and noticeably those jobs that are likely to get you promotion. Time is well spent on any jobs that enhance your status.

    2 Don't work in a disorganised mess. In particular, keep a tidy desk. It wastes time searching for the required papers amongst a muddle.

    3 Use no more time on a job than is strictly necessary to do it properly. There is no prize for being super fastidious. That loses both time and valuable energy.

    4 Do have a well-kept priority list. Then you will know

the jobs that must be undertaken before all the less important ones. To rely on one1s memory can be both frustrating and time wasting.

5 Be on time for all appointments. Starting a meeting on time will generally mean ending on time. Also, for meetings do have an agenda - that concentrates the mind and helps to stop participants wandering off into time wasting and pointless territory.

6 Keep a clear and easy to understand diary. Time can be so easily lost if you have two appointments away from your workplace. It is annoying to find that after the first appointment you have a long wait for the next one. There is not enough time to go back to the office. There is time to make some mobile `phone calls. You could well be wasting precious time in the middle of the working day. The remedy is this - carefully arrange appointments with the aim of saving time between appointments. 7 Keep routine work to a minimum. Do it at the less busy time of the day or even spend a little time at the end of the working day to bring it up-to-date. That`s self-inflicted overtime, but well worth doing. That is the sign of someone really wanting to be well organised and looking for promotion.

8 There are certain jobs that can be done outside of normal working time to ease the pressure on working time. For example, make sure that your car is full of petrol so that you don`t have to waste time whilst going to an appointment away from your workplace. Now, that last sentence illustrates a beneficial way of saving working time and it should be used as a model. Think about it and many other time saving ideas will come to mind.

An observation - as the old song says, "Time waits for no one"...and that includes YOU.

OBJECTIVES 17 – DEVELOP A GOOD MEMORY. IT SAVES TIME AND SHOWS YOU KNOW YOUR JOB

A good memory is both a timesaver and it shows that you undoubtedly know your job. A bad memory creates unnecessary work as you have to research virtually every move - you look incompetent and it shows you as someone who hasn`t a proper grasp of your job. You will appear woolly, aimless and dim - not promotion material. It is not necessary to have one of the best memories in town. You must train yourself to remember all the main facts and figures of your work. You needn`t worry that you haven`t that super memory - who has? To have a memory a little above the average one possessed by the man in the street is sufficient. But, and here is a necessary qualification, you must retain or learn to retain the information that will help you with your job. With that asset, your diary containing all appointments and your priority and follow up lists you will be well - prepared for the promotion push. To pack or try to pack your brain/memory with too much information will have the reverse outcome - you will forget far more than you will remember. A tip - useless information is useless in the brain, you are unlikely ever to have the need to recall it.

The following suggestions will help to improve your memory. Select the ones that suit your own style of working and concentrate on them:

1 The memory improves by use. You will find that by using it to remember the most obvious parts of your work you will increase its efficiency. You will begin to recall items that were often forgotten. So, use your memory but don`t overload it.

2 The memory works better when you are really interested in a subject. It follows that if you are interested and keen on your work (as you are now) it will be easier to recall facts and figures. Of course, it is obvious that if you have little or no interest in a subject you will have no reason to think about it. You glance at a subject that does not interest you, you turn away and that`s

that. It is dismissed from your thoughts. Remember this - the more involved and interested you are in your job the easier you will be able to recall information required.

3   Without any association memorisation would be nearly impossible to perform. Association means linking (associating) one matter with another. As an example, look at the house that you live in. You immediately think of the family and that brings back memories of all the good times, which brings back thoughts of Christmas, birthdays, et al. That`s true association. Look at the house on the opposite side of the road to your own house. It`s just a house, but if of similar design it will remind you of your house, little more. To you it doesn`t have all the love and care that you have lavished on your own home - different front garden, a different colour paintwork, the brown curtains are poor compared with the yellow ones of home...it is just another house without all the visual associations of your house.

4   Concentration and observation. Concentrate on the subject that you want to remember, observe any unusual features and associate it with its surroundings...That will help to create a vivid impression in your mind. Do not just look. Let the picture form in your mind; once powerfully painted it will not be too difficult to recall in the future. It will help if you remember just one meaningful aspect and that will bring back to mind the rest of the picture.

5   One of the greatest destroyers of memory is worry. It fills the mind and there is little room left for any other influences. The first influence to be totally or partially destroyed will be memory. It is important that if you are a worrying type you must try to decrease that destroyer – before it destroys you (OBJECTIVE 12). At the very least endeavor to lessen worrying influences in your day-to-day working life. In place of worry get interested, get positively involved in your job and in life generally. From that firmer base you will be able to improve both your memory and your chance of promotion.

It is not intended that you rigidly adopt the above ideas. As with all the suggestions given in these pages it is your choice as to which best suits your way of working. Furthermore, all suggestions are put forward so that you think through the various proposals made and build on them with your own ideas. Ponder on my suggestions and your own thoughts will throw out other ideas. That is one of the justifications for putting this book before you - to get you thinking of ways to achieve promotion. That brings back – **NOTHING HAPPENS UNLESS YOU MAKE IT.**

OBJECTIVE 18 - YOU MUST SAY "NO" IN A PLEASANT MANNER

This OBJECTIVE must be strictly obeyed...when dealing with the boss!

Very often you will have to reply in the negative and say, "no" and that may upset the recipient of the refusal. Sadly, you can`t please everyone. In fact, you should never hear yourself saying "yes" when in your own interest you should be saying "no". Many of us are too shy to disagree and that is often our downfall. It is essential that you learn to say "no" and to say it in a pleasant manner. Here is a lesson to learn - there is no disgrace in turning down a proposal or a proposition that is clearly not for you. Look at it this way - you are not being negative, you are being positive in your own interest and refusing to do something that will harm you. It may well show you in a strong light, as someone who first and foremost looks after his own. Not to do so will have, to you, two disadvantages - the actual disapproval and the way that it is given. Those two factors may annoy the recipient and from which your relationship with him may never recover. For example, to rudely say "no" to an offer which you had, perhaps unwittingly, given every indication that you would accept, would upset the offeror on two scores.

A reason why persons hate disagreeing is that most of us have the desire to be liked and will go to great lengths to achieve that aspiration. Sadly, in your workplace you must disregard/ignore whether you are hated or not. Clear your mind of such nonsense and do and say as circumstances dictate. Say a pleasant "no" when needs be. A show of credible independence is a sure double plus when promotion time arrives.

Here are some ideas that may help you to soften the blow when dissenting:

1 Look up the word "no" in a dictionary. You will find that it means denial, refusal, disagreement, dissent...and those are the reasons why you should avoid saying "no" when turning down a proposal. It can so easily rankle in the other person's mind. It is a hard and killjoy word.

It is not an easy exercise to avoid saying "no". Remarks that can usefully be made are, "Thanks, but that is something that I couldn't do...", "A good idea, but not one that suits me...", "That's kind of you, but it's not for me...". You get the idea, a polite yet firm "no". Always follow the refusal by the reason why it has to be a refusal. That will help to show that the refusal is an honest one.

2 Start the conversation that contains a refusal with a sincere compliment. That will set the scene for the refusal, although it is not an easy exercise to undertake. As examples, when you refuse to play golf on a specific date on the invitees home course. "I've played Heathstone and you have a wonderful course. I'd love another game there but...", "In certain circumstances your excellent proposal would suit but...", "I just love all your paintings. You must be very proud of them. I haven't any wall space at home for another painting. Sorry...". A general compliment softens the blow.

3 When refusing an invitation. This takes (1) and (2) above a step further. Always give a reason why it can't be accepted. As they say, gild the lily. It must be an honest reason; if not that, it must be one believable! If at all possible it will help to keep goodwill by suggesting another date.

4 Refusing to give a donation to charity. You must not

appear a skinflint. Work along these lines, "We always support The Barns Hospice - have done so for years. I`m have to say that we have already given our yearly allowance to them". Of course, you can only use this refusal if it is true.

    5 A collection of some "do`s" and "don`ts". DO - act gracefully, always be pleasant, put yourself in the other man`s shoes, be truthful (as possible). DON`T - be aggressive, raise your voice, be rude or swear, be personal, bring another person`s name into the proceeding

OBJECTIVE 19 - YOU MUST CONTROL STRESS OTHERWISE IT WILL CONTROL YOU

It is difficult to define stress. It is an emotional or physical strain or tension. It causes anxiety and/or nervous tension. It other words, it wears you out, makes you jittery, bad tempered, touchy and tired/drained. It is a disability that "takes it out of you". That is why it is so necessary to control it. It will ruin your working and nonworking life. It will ruin your health.

From the last paragraph you will realise that stress is very dangerous. It can knock you sideways.

IF YOU SUFFER FROM STRESS OR HAVE REASON TO BELIEVE THAT YOU DO, YOU MUST WITHOUT DELAY CONSULT YOUR DOCTOR. THERE IS NO ADVICE THAT I CAN GIVE OR AM QUALIED TO GIVE THAT WILL BE OF MEDICAL HELP TO YOU. ALL I CAN DO IS TO ENDEAVOUR TO HELP YOU TO TRY TO AVOID STRESS

It will help to keep stress away if you thoroughly know your job and consistently do it well, get on with your boss and with all persons that you come into contact with whilst at work, have faith that you are going to be promoted, have a happy home life and enjoy your hobbies...Of course, we all aim for those ideals. Fine, but to live a life completely free of stress envisages an ideal world and, sadly, we do not inhabit that planet. Therefore, it is necessary to look at our lives and to do our best to avoid the most harmful stress. Consider how the following ideas may help you:

1 The first advice has been stated many times in these pages as it is the overriding factor leading to promotion/success. It is this - you must thoroughly know your job. Doing a job that you don't really understand creates stress, there is no doubt about that. You are on tender hooks. Will you make a costly mistake? Will you let your boss down? Will you get the sack? These thoughts are always in the back of your mind. "I'm failing and I'm not going to get promotion". All these problems and more can cause worry and stress. So, it is vital that you thoroughly know your job. No ifs; no buts - no excuses, that advice must be obeyed.

2 You must know and respect your own weaknesses and limitations. This is linked with (1) above. Read again OBJECTIVE-2.

3 Don't work too hard. In this context "too hard" means excessively, too long hours with little or no home life, no hobbies...(OBJECTIVE-6). A tip - you must never work to impress. Work sensible hours so as to get your work satisfactorily completed.

4 Don't lose your temper, get agitated, want to "knock someone's block off" or similar. Words and actions of that nasty nature put your blood pressure up and harm you, no one else. Remain calm. Say what you feel and say it clearly and calmly.

5 Delegate work as far as possible, particularly if you are overloaded. Make sure that you keep the jobs that matter and that will help your promotion prospects. Do not delegate jobs that you should be seen doing and which may help another person's promotion chances. That may seem a little harsh, even unkind - it is, but everything is fair in love, in war...and when seeking promotion.

6 Don't take work worries home. That is not easy not to do. If you have a very significant worry that may mean loss of your job or you may be demoted discuss it with your

wife/partner - for it could harm her interests as much as ours. As is said, a trouble shared is a trouble solved. A discussion is unlikely to solve the problem but it could well throw new light on it and ease the burden on you. However, do make it a rule to keep insignificant and "office chatter" away from home.

7 Don't take work home unless it is absolutely vital to do so. As an example, to prepare papers to meet a deadline that otherwise would not be met.

8 Enjoy your home life and hobbies. Create security and happiness outside of the workplace. That is a (near) perfect way to keep stress to an absolute minimum.

20 A SET BACK COULD RUIN YOUR CHANCE OF PROMOTION UNLESS TREATED AS A LESSON <u>AND NEVER FORGOTTEN</u>

This is a somewhat worrying and depressing OBJECTIVE, so let's start it with a lesson that will lift the gloom.

A set back is only one of life's trials, it is generally caused by a mistake or, sometimes, by a stroke of bad luck. It is placed in your way for a purpose. The purpose is this - to teach you a lesson and, if you are wise, you will learn from that lesson. Thereafter, you should never make the same mistake again. So, looking at the big picture it is just part of life's interesting fabric and is as essential as a lucky break. Stop for a moment, reread and think about the last four sentences. They will help you to put a bad spell into the proper perspective.

A set back is rarely a disaster. Repeat - it is not a disaster and certainly not the final catastrophe that we all secretly dread. Nevertheless, there is a proviso. It can become a grave stumbling block if you let it. If you are still not convinced that a set-back is only a blip in the way of the world, cast your mind back to your last bad patch which, at the time, you thought proclaimed the end of your world. It was no such tragedy. You are still here and it is a certainty that you still want to do your best at your job and win promotion.

So, do not think any more silly nonsense. A set back is a lesson to learn - a mere ripple in your career.

It is always wise to prepare a defence if it is believed that an attack may be mounted against you. A set back is an attack on your career. Consider the following ideas and keep the one/s that suit your style of working in mind for use when (not "if") you are attacked by a setback:

1 The worse rarely happen. How many of those dreaded disasters of yesterday took place? Few, if any, is the most likely answer. It follows that you must not worry about something that may never happen. A lesson to learn - don't worry that a set back may come along, you are now fully prepared to tackle it and discard it in the dustbin of bad dreams.

2 You must be able to smile in the face of a set back. That, you may be thinking, is something that you just couldn't do. Look at it this way. You are thankful for a success. Equally, you should be thankful (maybe a little less so!) when a set back comes along as it will teach you a most valuable lesson. A mistake has been identified and won't (shouldn't) be allowed to happen again. The next move is to identify the mistake, put it right if possible and then to carry on with your job/career with that little extra expertise under your belt. Are you likely to get that promotion without the valuable lessons taught by set backs? This section of this OBJECTIVE will help to blow away the gloom associated with set backs.

3 All persons possess a deep reservoir of both physical and mental strength. When needed you will automatically draw on that reserve. You see, nature has given you a good start and it is your hands to build on that foundation.

4 A thought to call to mind when a set back appears on the horizon is this - difficulties are made to overcome. If that isn't true they are made to stop progress and to destroy success. We know that not to be true. They are, like those frightening fences on the Grand National course, obstacles to, figuratively speaking, jump over and gallop away to (hopefully) win the race.

Just temporary impediments virtually ignored by those determined to win the race (promotion).

    5 Never think of a set back as a failure. Permanently dismiss from your mind the idea that you may fail. Put in that void a strong belief that when you have a set back you will easily get over that little snag. You are not preparing yourself negatively for a set back, you are doing it positively so that a minor temporary glitch is followed by a confident move forward.

    A reminder - When a set back comes along don`t be hasty and rush into wrong decisions. Remain calm and retain your confidence in the future. I always say that you may lose everything but always hold on to your confidence.

THE CONCLUSION

    I do hope that these OBJECTIVES have taught you some valuable lessons that will help to get you that cherished promotion. Always keep in mind that the best advice in the world will not get you promotion. It is how you use that advice that is the final decider. After you hear "I am promoting you" continue to recall the motto that helped you get that promotion

NOTHING HAPPENS UNLESS <u>YOU</u> MAKE IT

www.ingramcontent.com/pod-product-compliance
Lightning Source LLC
Chambersburg PA
CBHW071543170526
45166CB00004B/1535